D1511972

Discovering
PERSONAL GOALS

Books and magazines can give you ideas about what you want your life to be like.

THE SELF-ESTEEM LIBRARY

Discovering
PERSONAL GOALS

Patricia M. Kramer

DISCARD

PUBLIC LIBRARY
EAST ORANGE, NEW JERSEY

THE ROSEN PUBLISHING GROUP, INC.

NEW YORK

Published in 1992 by The Rosen Publishing Group, Inc.
29 East 21st Street, New York, NY 10010

First Edition
Copyright 1992 by Patricia Kramer

All rights reserved. No part of this book may be reproduced in any form
without permission in writing from the publisher, except by a reviewer.

Printed in Hong Kong
Bound in the United States of America

Library of Congress Cataloging-in-Publication Data

Kramer, Patricia M.
    Discovering personal goals/ by Patricia M. Kramer.—1st ed.
    (The Self-Esteem Library)
    Includes bibliographical references and index.
    Summary: A discussion of the value of goal setting as a way to
succeed, exploring what goals are, how to set them, and how to
achieve them.
    ISBN 0-8239-1277-9
    1. Goal (Psychology)—Juvenile literature. 2. Success—Psychological
aspects—Juvenile literature. [1.Goal (Psychology) 2. Success.] I.Title.
II.Series.
BF504.3 K72 1991
153.8—dc20
                                    90-28777
                                        CIP
                                        AC

Contents

Introduction

"If we believe in ourselves and are willing

to work toward our dreams, we will achieve them."

As children we grow up believing that our dreams will come true. For years we pretend, imagine, and daydream about what our lives will be like. Along the way to adulthood we have to figure out how to make our dreams come true. Sometimes good things just happen to people. Things turn out just the way they want them to. Some people call that fate. Others call it luck. You've heard people say: "Some people have all the luck." Others say: "It's in the stars." But for most of us, our lives will be a mixture of good and bad.

No one can say for sure whether the stars or luck have any real impact on our lives. Some believe that only people can make things happen. They believe that we are in control of our lives. By being positive, believing in yourself, and setting goals, you can have what you want. You can make things happen just the way you want. You can begin this very moment by being positive and believing in yourself. And you can start setting goals that will point you in the right direction. That is what this book is about. **Setting goals.**

A positive attitude and belief in yourself can go a long way toward making the life you want.

Daydreams can be a way to explore what you want in the future.

Chapter 1
Daydreams

"Don't be afraid to dream."

Do you sometimes daydream when you're supposed to be paying attention? Do you daydream when you are supposed to be doing something or thinking about something else? Probably. We all do. We start daydreaming when we are very young. Our early daydreams were based on what we saw and heard around us. They probably started when we began the games of "Let's pretend." You remember when you played house or maybe you played doctor. You dreamed about the roles and what they would be like. They were daydreams. Different from the kind of dreams that you had when you were asleep. Those dreams you could not control.

Your daydreams are very personal. They're yours and no one else's. You can share them with others if you choose. You can keep them very private, all to yourself. Some people say that daydreaming is a waste of time. The good thing about daydreaming is that you can do it all alone. And you can do it whenever you want and wherever you want. It can even be a way to begin exploring your future. Let your imagination run wild. Think of all the things that you want to have happen in your life.

Let yourself begin to daydream. Here are some things you may want to daydream about: (Maybe you have already thought about some of them.)

1. What do I want to learn? Do I want to go to college or trade school? Do I want to go to graduate school after college—law school? Medical school?
2. What do I want to do as a career?
3. What stands in my way of pursuing my career goals?
4. Where do I want to live? In the city or the country? Big city or small city?
5. What will I look like in five years, ten years? (You can keep going until you see yourself as far into the future as you want. Will you look like your parents or your grandparents?)
6. What kind of fun or hobbies will I enjoy?
7. What can I do to make the world a better place to live?
8. Will I get married? Have a family?
9. What would I like different in my life one, two, three, four, five years from now?

The difference between a dream and a goal is the act of doing. The dreamer imagines. The goal setter acts. A dream remains a dream only if you fail to take

Wishing for things does no good unless you act to make your wishes possible.

the steps to achieve something more. That doesn't mean that all dreams will come true. Some dreams are just harder to make real than others. Some dreams you have less control over.

We all have different kinds of dreams. We have our personal dreams—what we want for ourselves like love and marriage. We have our career dreams—our self-fulfillment. We dream of what we want to be, what job we want. But some of us also have dreams that are part of the fate of others. For example, you may be deeply committed to an *ideal* or a *vision* of the way the world should be. Your dreams may be for world peace or food for the hungry. You may care about the problem of shelter for the homeless. Or you may want to work toward *humane* treatment for all animals. Those dreams can become goals for you as well. You can decide to work for any of those causes. The right dreams at the right time can give you strength to help them come true. The right dreams can inspire you to go on when you feel like giving up. When you believe in a dream, you believe in yourself and your ability to make it come true.

Maybe you have never thought seriously about any of these things. Maybe you've said to yourself, *"I'll worry about my future later. I'm young. I want to have fun now."* But there will come a time when you want to begin planning for your future. There will come a time when you want to set goals for yourself. That time may come sooner than you think. Since most plans must be set in motion long before a goal is reached, that time might be now. Make short-term goals to help you reach long-term goals.

Instant Gratification

It is only on television or in the movies that people get what they want or solve problems in thirty minutes or an hour. It seems that no matter what the problem, the actors always resolve it easily. They always get what they want—no matter what it is—in a very short time. Maybe some of us have come to believe that is the way it is in the real world. We now want *instant gratification.* That means we want what we want and we want it *now.* We don't want to wait. We don't want to work for it or plan for it.

Well, life is not like that. Most people have to work hard and sometimes wait a long time before they get what they want. Most of us have to do a lot of planning just to figure out what we really need. Then we have to plan how we are going to get it. Most of us have to set goals and work toward reaching them before we get what we want.

When thinking about who you really are, making lists of your strengths and weaknesses can help to clarify your ideas.

Chapter 2
Who Are You?

"To reach your goal, you must know yourself."

Before you can begin to think about your future and who you want to be, you have to know who you are. Knowing who you are will also help you to know more about the things you'll want to do as you grow older. Understanding more about your needs may also help you know what makes you act. You may want to explore some of your emotions. Here are some exercises that might help you know a little more about yourself. Try doing them on a separate piece of paper.

Write down five things that make you:
　　1. angry: For example: People who are cruel to animals.
　　2. sad: The homeless
　　3. happy: Being with good friends.
　　4. tense: Tests.
　　5. relaxed: Lying on the beach.

List ten emotions that you felt in the last week and why you felt that way.
For example: Scared. I was scared when I watched a horror movie on TV. Relieved. I was relieved when I got a B on the science test.

Finish these sentences and see how much you learn about yourself:
What I want most out of life is......
The people who are most important to me are......
I like being around people who are......
I feel good about myself when......
I am interested most in......
The biggest mistake I ever made was......
I would be happy if......
One thing I would like to change about me is......
One thing I would like to change in my life is......
One thing I would change about the world is......
One goal that I achieved is......
One goal that I didn't accomplish was......
I am happiest when......
I feel sad when......
I get angry when......

My Strengths

You also may want to consider the good qualities and skills that you have. Once you know some of your talents, you may discover which ones will help you meet your goals. Before you can be successful, you must first identify your strengths so that you'll know what resources you have. Then you can begin to develop your plan for personal growth.

On a separate sheet of paper, list ten positive qualities you have. First, be sure to give yourself permission to brag.

Next list all your skills or talents. For example: creativeness, writing ability, skill with numbers.

What Motivates Me?

To set a goal and reach it, you must know what *motivates* you. What moves you to action? What does it take to get you going? Each of us reacts differently to events around us. For some people, money may be the only thing that interests them. The thought of having money to spend moves them to get things done. If we know we're getting paid, we may start and finish a project quickly. For others friendship, having fun, getting an education may be what interests them. Some young people want to get higher grades to get into a good college. Others want to go to college so they can get a better job later. *On a separate piece of paper, list all the things that motivate you.* Spend some time thinking about it. Once you discover what moves you to action, it will be easier to reach your goals.

The old saying "Like mother, like daughter" may not be true when it comes to interests and goals.

Chapter 3

Family Environment and Goals

Borrowed goals usually don't work.

Our parents and our family life affect our future. We become who we are through *heredity*—those traits that we inherit from our parents. We also set standards for ourselves based on our *environment*—those things that surround us as we grow up.

Sometimes it is hard for our parents to realize that we may not want the kind of life that they wish for us. Many parents want their children to do the things that they themselves were not able to do.

Sometimes they try to set goals for their children by letting them overhear talk about what they want for them. For example, a parent says, "I know my son will follow in my footsteps; he's going to be a doctor," or, "She is so smart; I know she will make honors this year."

Boys and girls learn about goal-setting differently. Parents often encourage their sons to set and reach goals, but not their daughters. They may teach their daughters that they should be wives and mothers and nothing else. Nothing is wrong with those roles, but the girls often don't learn that they are capable of playing many other roles if they wish. As a result they may believe that their needs are less important than those of others. Often a young woman's self-esteem is so low that she never tries to set or reach goals.

Your parents may have had conditions that you had to meet in order to be loved or accepted. If so, you may not know how *to make decisions* or plans of your own. Many children are expected to live up to someone else's ideals. When that happens they sometimes rebel or even fail on purpose. If that has happened to you, you may be afraid to set goals for yourself. You may fear the loss of your parents' love if you make decisions on your own. You may fear their anger. Without being disrespectful to your parents, let them know that you must start being in charge of your own life.

Borrowing Goals

Sometimes we decide to borrow a goal and use it as our own because people we love, like, respect, or even fear suggest that it is the right one to have. For example: *What if you have a friend who is selling drugs and making a lot of money. He tells you that if you ever want to get out of the poor neighborhood, you had better sell drugs too. If that becomes your goal, you may temporarily have money, but you will end up with nothing but trouble—if you survive the drug wars and killings.*

When you pretend to have a goal to please someone else, you may miss out on setting your own goals. If you set goals only to please others, you have to take whatever comes. Most likely it will not be what you want. You have to lead your own life, or someone else will try to do it for you. If you do not set your own goals, you will have no choices in your life. If you take on goals that do not fit in with your own beliefs, you probably won't reach the goals that you do set— that is, if you set any at all.

For now you may have to do what others believe is right. As a young adult, however, you will have to make decisions about your future. If you are always trying to fit in or act the way others do, you may have trouble believing in yourself. When you have self-doubts it becomes difficult to make plans for your own future. If you don't find a way to begin making plans now, you may never have a life of your own. So start letting those around you know that if they tell you what to do or how to live your life and it doesn't feel right, you are going to have to say, "No."

Borrowed goals usually don't work. They can be harmful. Some young people have actually killed themselves because they could not live up to someone else's expectations. They thought they were supposed to be perfect, and they just couldn't be. No one can. **THERE IS NO SUCH THING AS PERFECTION!**

Working together toward a common goal leads to success and mutual satisfaction.

Chapter 4
Sharing Goals

"Mutual interests can make a relationship last."

Many times good friends share some goals. That may be what attracts each to the other. For example, John joins a stamp-collecting club to learn as much as he can so that he can start a serious collection. He meets George in the club, and they become friends because of their similar goals. Friendships like that can last a lifetime or as long as there are similar interests.

Sometimes people marry because they share similar goals in life. If or when their goals change, they may lose interest in each other and grow apart. That is one reason many people get divorced.

23

Sharing similar interests and goals may not be the most important part of a relationship, but it can be the reason it lasts. Too often people grow apart because they no longer have anything in common. Think about that when starting a new relationship—no matter what kind. Try to find out as much as you can about a person before getting involved in a close relationship. See how much your goals and values are similar. Opposites do attract sometimes, but when the first attraction begins to fade nothing may be left if there are no shared goals.

Discussing your goals with family and friends can help to clarify them.

Chapter 5
What Is a Goal?

"A dream becomes a goal when you start to make it

come true."

All of us have dreams about the future and what we want. It is assumed that all of us have goals too. It's just that some people don't know the difference. A dream is something you think about. A goal is something you are willing to work toward achieving. You've probably heard the saying, "He's a dreamer." You don't take a dreamer very seriously. But your goals shape who you are and who you will become. Your goals determine what you will be and where you will go with your life. When you have goals, people have respect for you. When you have goals, you have respect for yourself.

Before you can become an artist or an illustrator you must practice drawing your ideas on paper.

A goal is something you want and are willing to take action to achieve. Most people want things, but many are not willing to work at getting them. Goals are symbols of the real things you will have one day if you're successful. When you set a goal, you are making an appointment with yourself. You are saying that you want certain things to happen at a certain future place and time. The actions you take between now and then will determine whether you reach your goals.

The artist or writer has a dream of painting a picture or writing a book. It remains only a dream until the first dab of paint is splashed on a canvas or the first word is written. Then the dream becomes a goal. Each brushstroke on canvas or word on a page brings the artist or writer closer to his goal.

If your dream is to become a great jazz pianist, you must spend many hours learning to play the instrument, and more hours listening to the performance of people who have achieved that dream.

If you want to be a veterinarian and help to make animals well, you must learn how their bodies work and what can make them sick.

Your goals must be reachable—pound by pound.

Chapter 6
Setting Goals

"Go after your goals slowly. Start small and work your

way up. Eventually you'll get there."

When setting your goals, there are many things to think about if you want to succeed. Reaching goals doesn't just happen. You must prepare. You must think of all the possible roadblocks. What will get in your way? What will help you succeed? Here are some factors that you may want to think about:

- **IMPORTANCE.** Compared to other goals, how important is this one?
- **EASE.** How easy is it to reach this goal? Compared to other goals, is this one easy to reach and keep?
- **CONFLICT.** Is this goal in conflict with any other goal?
- **TIME.** How much time has been spent thinking about this goal? How much time will I have to put into reaching this goal?
- **SUPPORT SYSTEMS.** Do I have the right *support systems* available?

Here are some questions that you may want to ask yourself before setting your goals. If you cannot answer them in a positive way, you may not be ready to start working towards those goals.

1. **Is it reasonable and realistic?** "Can I really achieve this?" Your goal must have a chance of succeeding. We often set unrealistic goals on purpose. Then when we fail, we can always say: "Well, it was just too tough."

2. **Is it stated in a positive way?** Set the goal in a positive way by saying, "I will," not "I can't."

3. **Is it measurable?** "How will I know when I've achieved this?" You must be able to know when you've reached your goal.

4. **Is it your goal?** Are you borrowing it from someone else? Are you doing it because someone else wants you to? Are you doing it to win someone over? Unless you are working toward your own goal, you have little chance of succeeding.

5. **Is it long- or short-range?** You must first set short-range goals before you can establish long-term ones.

6. **Is it in line with your own values?** You cannot work toward a goal based on values that you do not believe in.

7. **Is it harmful to yourself or anyone else?** If it is, it will be self-destructive. It may be impossible to reach, too.

8. **Is it okay with others who may be involved?** Have you checked it out to see if they are willing to help? Have you asked if they want to be involved?

9. **Is there a trade-off?** Am I willing to give up something to reach this goal?

As you can see, it is not easy to set or reach goals. Here are some more ideas that may help you to work to achieve success.

1. **If you have more than one goal, combine them and work on them together as a project.**

2. **Work with someone who has the same goals.** It is sometimes easier to have another person to give you support and inspire you.

This father's goal of having a major league player in the family may not be realistic.

Be prepared to accept partial success. You can't hit the bull's-eye every time.

3. **Try to imagine the goal already reached.** The more clearly you can see your goal, the easier it will be to reach.

4. **Make your goal very specific.** If it is unclear in your mind, it will never be reached.

5. **Write down everything that motivates you toward reaching your goal.** Then list everything that gets in the way. Concentrate on what can help you. Try to remove the *obstacles*.

6. **Develop visual and written supports.** Write messages to yourself that will support you. Keep pictures around of people who have reached goals.

7. **Develop support systems.** You can't do it alone. You can never get it all together by yourself. We need people in our lives. Don't be afraid to ask for help. We don't have all the resources our-selves. We may not even know what resources we need without other people showing us or helping us.

8. **Remember that change does not happen overnight.** Goals may be areas of your life that you want to change. They may also be things that you have never done before. It takes time, so be patient.

9. **Brainstorm—alone or with others.** *Brainstorming* is looking at every possible problem, solution, or resource. In other words, explore everything that might help to set and reach goals. Brain-storming is a good way to come up with ideas, viewpoints, and options.

10. **Select a goal that is challenging.** What may be easy for one may not be comfortable or challenging to another. It is more rewarding to accomplish a difficult task than something easy.

11. **Be sure now and then to ask yourself if the struggle to reach the goal is worth it.** Every few months, ask yourself some tough questions. Then ask if you are still happy with your choice. It may be that you are no longer willing to pay the price of pursuing that goal. You may have to look for a new one or you may want to redirect the focus of your search.

Plan your goal the way you would plot a route to your destination.

Chapter 7
Identifying Goals

"We choose our tomorrows by the goals we select."

What if you wanted to take a trip but didn't know where you wanted to go? Do you think you could get there? Probably not. What if you walked into a store to buy something and suddenly forgot what you wanted. Would you be able to buy it? You can't set or reach goals if you don't know what you want or where you're going. So you must do some exploring. You may need to do some soul-searching. You need to look at your life and decide what is important. That doesn't mean forever. It only means for now. Goals can and will change all during your life.

Working toward a goal is like traveling in a car. If you don't turn on the motor, you'll never get there. Once started, you may at times go in the wrong direction, but at least you're moving. Even after you know what you want, you have to find a way to keep the motor running. Then you have to learn how to keep going in the right direction. Once you get the hang of it, you can get just about anywhere you want to go.

Let's look at how you can identify, set, and reach the goals you want to achieve. First, what are they? You probably have many goals for different parts of your life. Here are some examples of the kinds of goals you might want to reach.

Relationships

I would like to make more friends this school year.

Career

I want to own my own service station.

Education

I want to go to a trade school to learn auto mechanics.

Personal Development

I want to be on time for school this year.

Leisure Time

I want to take karate lessons this year.

Make a chart on a separate piece of paper of all the goals that you would like to reach, whether realistic or not. Your chart should have many headings.

1. The goal.
2. Is it a short-range or long-range goal?
3. Skills you need to reach the goal.
4. Skills you have to achieve the goal.
5. Resources you need.
6. Support system (if you need others to help).
7. How long it will take to reach the goal.
8. How you will know if you reach your goal.
9. Date completed.
10. What happened as a result of reaching your goal.

After you have identified your goals, play them back in your mind over and over again. Soon you will be able to *focus* completely on achieving them.

Chapter 8
Time Management

"Time. We can't see it or touch it, but we all wish we had more of it."

If you live to be 78, you will have about 28,000 days and 660,000 hours to reach your goals from the day you are born. You have 10,080 minutes a week and 8,736 hours a year to reach your goals. It sounds like a lot, but that's if you work 24 hours a day. In reality, most of us have very little extra time to spend working toward our goals. That is why it is so important to use your time wisely.

It may be a good idea to set up a time management program to help yourself. Keep a record of how you spend your time. Once in a while ask yourself, *"Am I spending too much time on this part of my plan?" "Is there something I am doing that wastes time?" "What am I not doing that I should be doing?"*

Here is a simple formula for setting up your time management program:

Trim off any wasted time.

Involve others for support.

Make your program easy to follow.

Examine your progress from time to time.

There are three things to learn to set up a good program. The most important thing is to learn to overcome *procrastination.* "Don't put off until tomorrow what you can do today." The second thing to learn is to set *priorities.* Know what is most important and do that before you do something else. And third, learn *self-discipline* or *self-control.*

Procrastination

How often do you put off doing things until another day? You look for any possible reason not to do something. You may be too tired that day. You've worked hard. You have a lot of homework. You're not in the mood to do that specific thing that day. If you use those excuses day after day, you may be procrastinating. You may think it is too hard. Maybe you are afraid that you'll fail if you try.

What usually happens is that we become overwhelmed and quit or don't try at all. All the steps needed to do the job sometimes seem like such a burden that you wonder if it is worth it. But remember how you feel when you don't get something done that you know you should. You drag around because you feel guilty. You feel stress and pressure. The great feeling that comes when you do get the job done affects everything you do too—but in a positive way.

Intelligent use of time is a valuable tool in reaching your goals.

On a sheet of paper, list all the things that you put off or found ways not to do this week. Then put down the excuses you used. Think about what it was that you were uncomfortable about. What might happen if you actually tried to do it?

Priorities

In setting priorities, you have to decide what is most important to you at the time. Decide on what must be done today. If it isn't done today, will it cause a problem or put someone out?

Then think about the things that can be put off until tomorrow, and finally the tasks that can be put off for a while. **On another sheet of paper, write the following headings:** (1) Actions that must be taken right away; (2) Actions that must be taken this week; and (3) Actions that must be done by _____. List all the tasks that you have been meaning to do but have put off. As you finish each one, check it off and write the date. Get in the habit of setting priorities by using this form. Things will not get done by themselves.

Your Success Plan

On a third sheet write down five goals you want to reach in the next five years. (It doesn't matter what kind of goal it is.) Then list two successes you want to have as a:

1. Teenager.
2. Young adult (20-25).
3. Young/middle-aged adult (26-45).

4. Middle-aged adult (46-59).

5. Young senior citizen (60-75).

6. Senior citizen (76 and over).

Self-Discipline/Self-Control

Self-discipline means being able to discipline yourself. That does not mean punish yourself. It means that you decide what is best for you and then set the right guidelines to follow. If you have a big test coming up, you stay home and study instead of going out with your friends.

A person with self-control controls how he or she feels and acts. You cannot control the way the rest of the world thinks or behaves. Others can do as they like, but you have direct control over your life. If you have a goal that you want to reach you must be in control and decide what you have to do reach that goal. Sometimes it may mean giving up something you want to do.

Working at a job can provide the funds needed to fulfill a goal of getting a college education.

Chapter 9
Trade-Offs

"Self-denial may be necessary to reach some goals."

When you have been successful at one thing, you probably had to give up something else to get it. That's called a trade-off. While doing one thing, you may not be able to do another. For example, if you are saving money for your future but one day decide to buy a motorcycle, then you have no more money. Of course you can earn more, but you have to start from scratch. What if you get a job to earn money for college? During that time you might miss out on spending time with your family, being with your friends, or going on a field trip with your classmates. Those are the hidden costs. They must always be weighed when you set a goal. Is money more important than family or friends? Or is going to college the most important thing to you now?

Another trade-off might be paying a lower or a higher price (not just in money) to reach a goal. Say you decide to wait to go to college so you can help your parents. You may pay more later. It may cost more in dollars, but it may also cost you in another way. For example, going to college at eighteen is different from going when you are thirty-five and have a family. The cost of holding a job and raising a family at the same time will be higher. You must decide what is more important to you. You must decide what you are willing to give up to get something else.

Self-denial may be necessary to reach some goals. You may have to free yourself from some activity that is less important to succeed at another, more important goal.

In Chapter 1 we talked about instant gratification, and how we are hardly ever able to get what we want at the moment we want it.

Instant gratification can be a serious *obstacle* to achieving your goals. Anything really worth achieving is worth waiting and working for.

Chapter 10

Fear of Failure

"When we strive for a difficult dream, we must be

prepared to fail."

Throughout your life you will have dreams about what you want to do and who you want to be. At times there will be obstacles that prevent you from reaching many of those dreams. But there's a big difference between putting aside a goal and being afraid to go after it for fear of failure. Some people are so afraid of falling flat on their face that they don't even try. They may get discouraged, panicky, and even depressed when that happens.

One way that we set ourselves up for failure is to put roadblocks in our path. For example, *saying that you want to go to college and then not going to class.* Setting impossible standards is another way we prevent ourselves from reaching goals. For example, *deciding*

Fear of failure can make you "trash" your goals and lessen your success in life.

that you want to go away to college when you know your parents cannot afford to send you and your grades are not good enough to get a scholarship. That is an unrealistic goal. If you do that often, nothing you ever do will be good enough. Then you decide to do nothing. Wanting to be perfect at anything can be crippling. People who fear failure don't know where to look to find meaning in their lives. They sometimes give up.

The great English poet Rudyard Kipling wrote: "We have forty million reasons for failure, but not a single excuse." He meant that thinking we are going to fail is a sure way to make it happen. There is no excuse for failure because we do not have to allow ourselves to fail.

The good news is that none of us was born with only one chance for success in life. We have many chances. You may have to search a little harder to find some of them. Understanding how you block yourself from reaching your goals may help you see a way past the wall you build against success.

Volunteering to take on a challenging task is a risk that can lead to important personal growth.

Chapter 11
Taking Risks

"Everything is sweetened by risk."

–Alexander Smith

If you want to reach your goals, you must be willing to take risks. Of course, you hope that the risk will pay off. You may have to give up something. You may have to admit you made a mistake in the past. You must be willing to accept feedback from others. And you may not always like what you hear. When you take a risk, you may also have to let go of some of your beliefs. It may be that some values or ideals that you held in the past don't work for you now. Risk-taking is opening yourself up to change. It means trusting or relying on other people. Many people find it hard to trust others. 49

To laugh is to risk appearing the fool,
To weep is to risk appearing sentimental,
To reach out for another is to risk involvement,
To expose feelings is to risk exposing your true self,
To place your ideas, your dreams before the crowd is to risk their loss,
To love is to risk not being loved in return,
To live is to risk dying,
To hope is to risk despair,
To try is to risk failure,
But risk must be taken, because the greatest hazard in life is to risk nothing.
The person who risks nothing does nothing, has nothing and is nothing.
He may avoid suffering and sorrow, but he simply cannot learn, feel,
change, grow, love, live.
Chained by his certitudes, he is a slave, he has forfeited freedom.
ONLY A PERSON WHO RISKS—IS FREE

—Anonymous

Accepting the Consequences

If you are willing to take a risk, you must be ready for the response from others. They may take advantage of you. They may not approve. Some may try to make you feel guilty. You may even be rejected by people who are important to you. You may have to confront them and tell them how you feel about what they're doing. You must even be willing to fail.

How to Be a Risk-Taker

First you must ask yourself these questions:

1. If I am unwilling to take the risk, what chance do I have of reaching my goal?
2. What is keeping me from reaching my goal?
3. What must I do now to take the risk?
4. What is the worst thing that can happen to me if I take this risk?
5. What will my life be like if I don't take the risk?
6. How will I feel about myself if I sit back and do nothing?

Next try to imagine what it would be like if you took the risk and reached your goal. Imagine what it would feel like to be a winner. Now say out loud the following (if you care what people think, do it when no one is around):

I have overcome my fear of taking risks.

I know there are chances to take, but I'm willing to take them.

I enjoy being a risk-taker.

I am a winner.

Remember, if you take no risk at all, you have zero chance of succeeding. When you take the risk, your chances of succeeding usually outweigh your chances of failing. Go for it.

Negative to Positive

You must try to turn negative thoughts into positive ones. Just because someone says, *"I can't imagine it"* doesn't mean that someone somewhere can't accomplish it. People said that about transplanting human hearts and about landing on the moon. Those

51

negative thinkers were proved wrong. Don't say anything is impossible. Maybe it has been impossible until now. Maybe you haven't been able to get As in school. Maybe you've convinced yourself that you can't. But why not say, "Until now I haven't got As, but next year I can." Change from, "It's impossible" to, "It's possible."

For example:

Don't say you were stupid to try...Say you had courage to take a chance.

Don't say you are a failure...Say you haven't succeeded yet.

Don't say you haven't done anything...Say that you have learned a lot.

Don't say you were a fool for believing in others...Saying you had faith in others.

Don't say you've been disgraced...Say you were willing to try.

Don't say you don't have it...Say you have to do something differently the next time.

Don't say you're all washed up...Say that now you have a chance to try something new.

Don't say you are inferior...Say you are not perfect. (Nobody is.)

Because you have failed once doesn't mean that you should give up. It means that you should try harder the next time. Failure doesn't mean you'll never make it. It just means it may take you a little longer. Failure doesn't mean that you don't know how to make decisions. It means that you have a chance to make another one. Failure is never final.

Anticipation and Worry

Anticipation and worry also play a great part in our lives. Anticipation is the feeling you have when you're waiting for something to happen. Sometimes the anticipation turns out to be more important or more exciting than the actual event or goal. For example, running a race may be more exciting than finishing it. Or the boat trip across the water to the island may be more fun than being there.

Too often, we waste time worrying about what might happen instead of focusing on ways to make things happen. Worry is one of the most wasteful emotions we have. It takes so much energy—energy that could be used to accomplish the goal. Think about the saying used by Alcoholics Anonymous, the group that helps people who are alcoholics:

> "Grant me the *serenity* to accept the things
> I cannot change,
> the courage to change the things I can,
> and the wisdom to know the difference."

Causes of Failure

Sometimes we fail because we keep waiting for the "right" time to take action. Don't wait. The time may never be right. Start now and work with whatever skills you have. You'll probably be able to improve your skills along the way.

There are many other reasons why we fail to reach a goal that we have set. Most of them are caused by

53

not starting out with the right attitude. Here are a few:

Lack of persistence.
Lack of imagination.
Lack of purpose. You cannot succeed if you don't have a
    definite goal.
Lack of "the right kind" of education.
Lack of self-discipline or self-control.
Fear of taking a risk.
Wrong selection of peers or people to help you
reach your goals.
Wrong selection of goal.
Lack of ability to concentrate.
Lack of excitement.
Lack of patience.
Inability to get along with others.
Dishonesty.
Believing you're always right.
Lack of common sense.
Lack of belief in yourself.

Some of these reasons may fit you. Can you think of reasons you have failed in the past. *On a sheet of paper, list at least five areas that may have caused you to stumble and fall.*

What If I Don't Reach My Goals?

"A quitter never wins and a winner never quits."

Not every goal you set works out the way you want it to. Events will occur that you can't control. For example, what if you plan to finish high school but a crisis at home forces you to drop out? You may have to go to work to help your family. All of a sudden your hopes of college go down the drain.

If your first plan doesn't work, come up with a new one as soon as possible. Start over. If you don't, you might give up. When you feel defeated, accept it as a sign that your plans were off track or need to be changed. Temporary defeat is not permanent failure. You're not beaten until you quit. If you give up before your goal has been reached, you may be a quitter.

Here are some questions that you can ask yourself at the end of the planned time period:
1. Why didn't I reach my goal?
2. Did I put enough effort into it?
3. Did I go about it properly? If not, what can I do differently next time?
4. Did I select the right people to help me?
5. Are my goals realistic? Am I aiming too high or too low?
6. Am I still interested?

You may also want to spend some time finding out how other people set and reached their goals. Talk to your parents, teachers, friends. Discuss their tactics with them. You may want to ask them such questions as:
1. How did you know what goals you wanted to set?
2. How did you go about setting them?
3. How did you know when you had reached them?
4. How did you feel after you had succeeded?
5. What did you do when you didn't reach your goal(s)?

You Can't Win Them All

Nobody has it all. It is impossible to have it all. No one ever does—but we often think that others do. The school jock and the prom queen may seem to have it all, but they really don't. They had just as much chance of losing as anyone else. But they probably set their minds on the things that were important to them and worked hard toward getting them. There will be a few people who seem to do better than you. Maybe things come easier for them. It's possible that they are smarter, faster, more creative, and even luckier than you. That's the way life is. So some people may pass you by in reaching their goals. We can't say that you shouldn't let that bother you. It probably will. We can say that envy and jealousy will get you nowhere. Being envious or jealous simply gets in your way. It's a waste of time that could better be spent planning to achieve what is important to you. *Envy* and *jealousy* may push you to do things that hurt you more than help you. Instead of being jealous of what others have, figure out what you really want. Then go after it. Work as hard as you can. Follow your heart some-times. And follow your head other times. It's hard always to know which path is the right one. There is nothing wrong with being a follower rather than a leader at times. Followers still have the opportunity to be successful.

Be as fair with yourself as you would be with someone else. You may find that you have not done so badly, and maybe you won't be so hard on yourself. We often judge ourselves too much and give ourselves less credit for our successes.

Chapter 12

Making It Happen

"When you are really ready to do something,

you will find a way and the means to do it."

You're not too young to begin thinking about what you want to be when you grow up. Dreaming, planning, thinking, searching, discussing, and questioning are all ways to start to explore your choices. You don't have to make any decisions yet.

There will be challenges throughout your life. No person and no books can tell you it will be smooth sailing. The sooner you understand that, the sooner you will be able to get on with your life. The sooner you will also begin to make plans for the things that you really want. Being yourself takes a lifetime. We never get it perfect. We are always discovering new things about ourselves that we never knew. No matter how you prove yourself, there will always be another test tomorrow to challenge you again.

This important piece of wisdom is inscribed on the tomb of an Anglican Bishop (1100 A.D.) in Westminster Abbey:

"When I was young and free and my imagination had no limits, I dreamed of changing the world.

As I grew older and wiser, I discovered the world would not change, so I shortened my sights somewhat and decided to change only my country.

But it too seemed immovable.

As I grew into my twilight years, in one last desperate attempt, I settled for changing only my family—those closest to me—but alas, they would have none of it.

And now as I lie on my deathbed, I suddenly realize:

*If **I HAD ONLY CHANGED MYSELF FIRST,** then by example, I might have changed my family.*

From their inspiration and encouragement, I would then have been able to better my country, and who knows,

I may have even changed the world."

If you have talent, training, and experience and you are willing to work hard, you can be successful. This book has been intended to suggest some ways to achieve your goals in life and ways to avoid making mistakes that would make your progress more difficult. An unknown poet knew how to make it happen:

"Only as high as I reach can I grow,
Only as far as I seek can I go,
Only as deep as I look can I see,
Only as much as I dream can I be."

Good luck to you on your road to success.

Like climbing a ladder, success is achieved one step at a time.

Glossary

brainstorming Offering ideas or suggestions to solve a problem. Let's *brainstorm* and see if we can come up with some new ideas.

creative Artistic and imaginative. He got the job in the art department because he was so *creative*.

decision-making The act of making up one's mind. The *decision-making* process is important when setting goals.

environment The conditions and circumstances that surround something. The *environment* she lived in caused her to be unhappy.

envy Desire for something that someone else owns. *Envy* can destroy a friendship.

focus To make something clearer. It is important to *focus* if you're going to have clear goals.

gratification Pleasure or satisfaction. His parents felt great *gratification* when he graduated.

heredity Traits passed from parents to children through genes. Because of *heredity*, she had a hearing problem.

humane Characterized by kindness. Animals have a right to *humane* treatment.

ideals Beliefs of how things ought to be. She had high *ideals* for her future.

jealousy Resentment of another. His *jealousy* was hurting their relationship.

motivation Encouragement to action. *Motivation* keeps us moving toward our goals.

obstacle Something that gets in the way. There were too many *obstacles* in the way of reaching the goal.

persistence Refusal to give up in the face of problems. Her *persistence* really paid off in her job search.

priority Actions placed in order of importance. I need to set *priorities* if I'm going to make the team.

procrastination Putting off doing something. *Procrastination* almost always keeps us from reaching our goals.

self-discipline Ability to control one's feelings or actions. She showed a lot of *self-discipline* when she stayed home studying instead of going to the party.

sentimental Showing tender, gentle, or delicate feelings. She was *sentimental* when she watched sad movies.

serenity Calmness or peacefulness. Peggy found *serenity* when she sat by the lake.

subconscious The part of the mind that is not fully conscious. The *subconscious* sometimes keeps people from being realistic about their goals.

support system Person or group of people who give encouragement or comfort when needed. We all need a strong *support system* to turn to when we are in need of help.

vision A mental image. Her *vision* was to see all living things treated humanely.

For Further Reading

Kramer, Patricia. *The Dynamics of Relationships. A Prevention Program for Teens and Young Adults, Book 1 and Book 2.* Equal Partners, Kensington, Maryland, 1990, 450 pages. This book, designed originally for schools, deal with such topics as Self-Esteem, Communication, Conflict, Dating, Love, Marriage, Sexuality, and Parenting. It is filled with information, stories, examples, and activities.

Lee, Mary Price. *Coping Through Effective Time Management.* The Rosen Publishing Group, New York, NY 1991.

McFarland, Rhoda. *Coping Through Self-Esteem.* The Rosen Publishing Group, New York, NY 1988.

Smith, Sandra Lee. *Coping with Decision Making.* The Rosen Publishing Group, New York, NY 1989.

Index

About the Author:
Patricia Kramer is president of Equal Partners, an educational consulting firm that conducts nationwide training programs, staff development, and workshops for schools, social service agencies, and national organizations. She has been a featured speaker at many national education conferences, been a guest on national radio and television shows, and been featured in many educational magazines and other national publications. Ms. Kramer has received the Golden Apple Award from the Foundation for Self-Esteem "for making an outstanding contribution toward the development and furtherance of self-esteem" and was recognized by the District of Columbia Association of Counseling and Development for outstanding "Program Development."

Photo credits:
Cover photo by Chuck Peterson
Page 24: Chris Volpe
All other photos by Stuart Rabinowitz.

Design and production by Blackbirch Graphics, Inc.

DISCARD

EAST ORANGE PUBLIC LIBRARY
Discovering personal goals
Jr.Dept. 158   / Kramer, Patricia M.,

3 2665 0009 7077 4